By Tim Ganley & Vie Binga

This book is dedicated to the legendary waterman Tom Blake, the Coast Guard all around the world, the Water, and all Life on and in it.

Preface

If you are holding this book in your hands, you either already know how much fun flat water (or recreational) stand up paddling is, or you are about to find out real soon.

Flat water stand up paddling is not just fun, it is also extremely easy, or at least, a lot easier than most people think it is, as long as it is performed properly.

Then the imminent question arises: If it is so much fun and so easy, why would you be writing a book on it?

The purpose of this book is dual:

First off, we are aiming to bring awareness to the inherently dangerous nature of flat-water stand up paddling. Yes, stand up paddle boarding, as strange as it may seem, can be dangerous and even fatal. It saddens us to report that lives have been lost due to improper use of stand up paddle gear or due to poor guiding skills. We strongly believe that with enough knowledge, education, proper instruction and skill development more and more people will safely enjoy this positively life-changing activity for years to come.

Secondly, we believe that like any other outdoor activity stand up paddling deserves respect and attention. The more you delve into its rich world and the more you become aware of its intricacies, the more fulfilling it will become for you and your friends. Imagine packing up a drybag with your camping gear and taking a trip across the Florida Keys.

The methodologies that we are giving you come from having taught various forms of paddle boarding to thousands of clients throughout the years. While keeping in mind that every one learns differently, we have chosen what we consider the most essential and the most practical.

We are going to keep this book as simple as possible. Our philosophy is that ignorance leads to complexity and fear, while understanding leads to simplicity and confidence.

A word of advice - General

Water activities are an assumed risk sport. You assume all liabilities for your participation. This book does not take the place of appropriate instruction in paddling, swimming and life saving techniques. It is the ultimate responsibility of the paddler to judge their ability and act accordingly. This is what we found, over the years, to work best for us in keeping our clients and friends safe while flat-water stand up paddling. You may have to add or subtract accordingly depending on your area and waterway.

A word of advice - For SUP Guides/Instructors

You cannot successfully teach anything you do not understand or believe in.

So, we highly recommend to continuously practice, practice, practice *proper* technique, your selves. Contrary to popular belief, practice does *not* make perfect. Practice makes permanent. Please, practice wisely...

An ongoing process...

This book will continue to improve and grow as the stand up paddling sport evolves. In the meantime, we would love to hear back from you on what worked and what did not. If you have a better way of performing one of the tasks or you have found a piece of gear that makes your life easy, please, let us know! Thank you for reading!

- Tim & Vie

November 2015

INTRODUCTION

A Very Brief History

Stand up paddling is an extremely old activity, as evidence dating back to 9,000 years ago suggests. However, it is only within the last few decades that paddle boarding has reemerged.

The reemergence of paddle boarding is due mainly to Thomas Edward Blake (March 8, 1902 - May 5, 1994) the most accomplished and least understood surf pioneer of modern times. According to Gary Lynch (Surfer Magazine, November 1989, Volume 30, Number 11) andthe Encyclopedia of Surfing (by Matt Warshaw) some of Blake's contributions include the first hollow-core wood paddle board, which was responsible for saving thousands of lives, first sailboard, waterproof camera housing, first surfboard fin and the torpedo rescue buoy, who's design is still in use today. He was born in Milwaukee, WI (a town very dear to my own heart.

Even though this book is not about Thomas Blake, we wish to point out that it is due to him that stand up paddle boarding and surfing are as widespread and popular today.

Today's Reality

"A life without adventure is likely to be unsatisfying, but a life in which

adventure is allowed to take whatever form it will, is likely to be short." - Bertrand Russell

So how do we find that balance in between "a fulfilling adventure" and "safety"? The answer is easier than we think as long as we recognize that it is really about a dynamic balance and not a crystalized set of rules that we must follow.

Everything that we do in life has an associated risk, anywhere from loss of gear to loss of life. A good way to think about risk is as the probability of "something bad happening" multiplied by the "severity of the outcome." In layman's terms, "how bad is bad going to be?"

To give you an everyday example, what is the risk of riding your bicycle in the city? How likely is it that you are going to get hit by a car? And in that case, how critical could the possible injury be?

What we are looking at here is a twofold process:

- Minimizing the likelihood of "bad things from happening."
- Assuming "bad things happened", minimizing the severity of the "negative outcome."

This twofold process is based on 2 types of fundamental parameters:

- Hazard Factors
- Safety Factors

If for every activity, for every scenario, we are able to identify these factors, then we can reduce the associated risk so we can continue to enjoy the excitement that our "adventure" offers us.

A "hazard factor" has the potential to harm. Hazard factors refer to:

- Environment (terrain, weather conditions, etc.)
- Equipment/gear (using improper gear for the conditions, etc.)
- People (lack of skills, poor behavior, etc.)

A "safety factor" has the potential to reduce damage. Safety factors refer to:

- Environmental Education
- Proper use of the right equipment
- Training
- Skill Development
- Protocols
- Judgment/Common Sense

When you are on the water, there are hazard factors and safety factors. We expect that after reading this book you will have enough knowledge to identify the former and increase the latter, respectively, in order to minimize the risk and turn every paddle board trip into a fun and rewarding experience for you and your friends!

How To Use This Book

This book is strictly targeting flat-water stand up paddling and guiding, in calm weather conditions under 18 mph with no lightning.

No prior knowledge of stand up paddle boarding techniques or gear is required, however, common sense is a prerequisite for reading, understanding and implementing the suggestions found in this book.

Understanding Gear

We are going to start by studying the gear that is essential for paddle boarding. What you are going to love, is that there is not really that much to talk about. It is not a "technical activity" such as climbing or scuba diving.

If you already own or have otherwise access to a paddleboard and/or other SUP gear, this book will help you understand and appreciate what your gear is best made for.

If you do not already have access to a paddleboard/gear, after reading this book you will be able to choose the board and gear that is best suited for your size, skills and needs.

Keep in mind that the stand up paddle board industry is still very new and changing very fast and there are almost no industry standards. What we are giving you here is the foundation that you need to be asking the right questions.

When it comes to paddleboards, it is important to remember 2 facts:

Fact #1: Not all boards are created equal.

Fact #2: There is no such a thing as "one size fits all."

Proper Technique

In the second section of the book we will go over essential skills such as proper stance, paddle strokes and muscle activation. Stand up paddle boarding, if performed right, will serve simultaneously as a great core strengthening and joint rehabilitating activity.

When it comes to proper paddleboard form, it is important to remember the following fact.

- Paddle boarding is an activity inherent to our human nature.

Safety Principles

Even though we believe safety is of the utmost importance, we need to have understood gear and technique first, so we can all speak the same language. In this section, we will cover the essential safety principles that you need to follow as a paddle boarder and also the principles that you need to adhere to when taking other people out on the water, whether friends, family or paying clients.

Keep in mind that if you are planning on incorporating stand up paddle board guiding into your business, you want to get as much practice (i.e. time on the water) as possible making your friends and family your "students" first.

When on the water, whether with paying clients or not, you must above all consider yourself a guide. Therefore, safety should always be your number one concern.

"Of the many dozens of medals, awards and trophies won by Blake, it was the statement made by the National Surf Life Saving Association of America that pleased him the most. It praised Blake for "the thousands of lives saved because of his inventive contributions in the interest of fellow human beings."

Code of Ethics

It is your responsibility as a stand up paddler and/or stand up paddle guide to respect and honor the water and all life on or in it, at all times.

A Note from Blake

"While on a board, either surf riding or paddling, one is truly free from land bound restrictions. For that hour, he is captain of his fate, of his miniature ship. The burden of city, school, job, as well as the cares and worries of the subconscious mind are erased and forgotten, until the tensions of living again build-up. The remedy again is obvious; go surfing. Next time you leave shore for some fun, look and listen for the muted voice of atom, the voice of the wave, the voice of the good earth, and you, too, may hear the drum beat. Those who have, it goes like this: "All is well.""

From the book "Tom Blake: The Uncommon Journey of a Pioneer Waterman

PART I

Chapter 1 - Your Board

Paddle Board Terminology 101

- **Hull –** The overall "body shape" of your board.
- **Nose (or Bow)** – The front end of the board.
- **Tail (or Stern)** – The back end of the board.
- **Deck** – The top surface of the board, where you actually stand on.
- **Deck Pad** – Refers to the material that is placed on the deck (whole deck or part of) to provide traction and cushion for the feet.
- **Bottom** – The part of the board that glides on the water.
- **Rails** – The sides or edges of the board.
- **Fin(s)** – At the bottom of the board, typically towards the tail.
- **Fin Box(es)** – The box(es) that house(s) the fin(s).

- **Handle** – For carrying the board. Typically, in the middle of the deck or slightly off center.
- **Leash Cup** – At the tail of the board where you attach the "small" end of your leash.
- **Air Vent** – Not all boards have them. Make sure you know if your board has one.

Paddle Board Architecture 101

Hull

There are typically 2 distinct types of hull:

- Planing hull
- Displacement hull

A paddle board with a planing hull is meant to "ride on top of the water", skim, across the water's surface, much like a traditional surfboard. Planing hull is very common for "all around" paddle boards, which require more versatility so that they can perform well in recreational paddling, doing fitness on the board and playing in waves.

A paddle board with a displacement hull is meant to "cut through the water, plowing through, displacing it", much like an outrigger canoe. Displacement hull is very common for "racing paddle boards" and "touring paddle boards", because it allows them to deliver higher speeds with less effort from the paddler.

Rocker

The rocker of the board refers to the curvature of the board and it is typically measured in terms of nose rocker and tail rocker.

To find these 2 measurements, turn your board upside down, so you are facing the bottom of the board. Take a straight piece of wood that is longer than your board and place it lengthwise on your board.

- The nose rocker is the distance of the piece of wood from the tip of the nose of your board.

- The tail rocker is the distance of the piece of wood from the tip of the tail of your board.

As a rule of thumb the more rocker the board has, the more playful it is on waves. A displacement hull board will typically have minimal rocker.

Nose

First off, the nose of the board is defined by the hull of the board, i.e. displacement versus planing. Then based on the hull, the dimensions of the nose and the rocker of the nose add to the intricacies of the board, i.e. best suited for paddle surfing, touring, fitness, all-around, etc.

As a rule of thumb, the more surface area the front of the board has, the more stability the board has.

Tail

The shape of the tail of the board can get very technical: pin tail, round tail, swallow tail, bat tail, square tail, etc.

As a rule of thumb, the more angular shapes allow for more pivotal and sharper turns. The rounder shapes allow for rounder and smoother turns. A wide square tail allows for more stability.

Deck

These can be domed, flat or recessed. As a rule of thumb, a dome shaped deckwith thinner rails allows for more volume to be displaced towards the center for added buoyancy and easier maneuvering in the waves. A flat deck with less rounded rails allows for less play in the waves and more stability.

Deck Pad

Most paddle boards, these days come with pre-installed deck pads. The material varies depending on the type and brand of the board. As a rule of thumb, dedicated fitness boards have smooth (no ridges or grooves) deck pads for added comfort during "floor" type poses. Also some "rental" and "soft-top" boards have a full deck pad covering the whole deck of the board, typically made of EVA (Ethylene Vinyl Acetate), an elastic, non-water-absorbent foam.

Bottom Contour

The shape of the bottom of the paddle board, allows water flow to be directed through the length of the board, depending on the primary target of the board, i.e. stability, maneuverability, or speed. Some of the common bottom contours are flat bottom, concave bottom, convex bottom, V-bottom, channel bottom.

As a rule of thumb, a flat bottom makes the board quick, loose and responsive. A convex bottom, whether towards the nose or the tail, forces the board to work harder to move because it has to plow through water rather than skimming on top of it. This design is useful in bigger surf, where speed is not an issue and control is more important. A concave bottom allows for more water flow to be contained through the length of the board, which causes more lift, less drag and increased acceleration through turns as well.

Rails

Without getting deep into the architecture of a board, there are two distinct types of rails, in general:Soft and Hard.

- Soft rails are "soft" to look at; they are rounded, transitioning very smoothly from the deck to the bottom of the board, without any hard edges.

- Hard rails (or down rails) are more squared off, transitioning from the top to the bottom in a more distinct manner. They may even form an edge (or angle) with the bottom.

As a rule of thumb, harder rails create more maneuverability and speed and softer rails allow for more stability. You should feel fairly stable with medium rails (the meeting point of the top of the rail and the bottom of the rail is in the middle of the rail) and still be able to turn in a tight radius.

Fins

Paddleboard fins come in all sorts of flex types, sizes, shapes and configurations. Fin architecture can get extremely technical and the more you standup paddle the more aware you will become of the characteristics of your fins. However, you can still have an awesome time on the water without understanding anything about your paddle board fins other than how to put them on and take them off.

Here are some facts that will help introduce you to the fabulous world of paddle board fins:

- A larger, heavier paddler needs a fin set with more surface area to provide more hold.

- Boards with wider tails or a lot of rocker require more fin area.

- Board with flatter rockers, thicker rails, deep channels, or narrower tails can get away with fins with a smaller area.

- Fins can be plastic, fiberglass, composite (such as hexcel), injection molded (such as nylon with fiber content), etc.

- Flex is the amount a fin will bend from the straight position. A fin with more flex will be forgiving loosening the board while a stiffer fin will respond better, improve speed and drive.

- Fins can have shorter base or longer base for more drive and acceleration. Base is the length of the fin where it meets the board. Fins with a smaller base will have a shorter turning arc.

- Fins can be of longer-profile (or depth) such as Dolphin style, or low-profile such as Trout style. The greater the depth the more hold, the shorter the depth the more a board will slide and release.

- A fin's sweep is the degree to which the tip extends beyond the fin's base. Fins with a large sweep will propel the board faster and remain fairly stable, but they will sacrifice some turning ability. Fins with a smaller sweep give the paddleboard a tighter turning radius, but they do not offer as much stability.

- Fins can be symmetrically foiled or asymmetrically foiled. Foil refers to the shape and geometry of the inside and outside faces of the fin. Foils directly affect the flow of water over the surface of the fin. Different foils create variations in water flow and have a direct link to the overall performance of the fin and the board.

- The fin's base can be inserted to the fin box through a nut and a screw, ball bearing, quick release, etc.

Fin Configurations

Different fin configurations include single fin configuration, twin fin, tri-fin, thruster, quad, etc.

- Single fin configuration favors the board when moving smoothly, encouraging gliding in a straight line, but not when moving abruptly. For more stability, it is recommended to move the center fin back a bit.
- The twin fin ranks high for maneuverability because one fin can act as the pivot point while the other spins around it. Also, the twin fin is also known for being very fast since it does not have a trailing center fin producing drag.

- A tri-fin board is only faster when it is pumped rapidly from rail to rail. The smaller outside fins encourage directional change, however, in a straight line, they produce drag.

- Thrusters blend the maneuverability of twin fins with the hold of single fins to create a new type of performance. The thruster setup can be arranged a few ways. The most common is to have three equal sized fins set up in a triangular pattern with the center one closest to the back of the board. The center fin is typically a double-foiled fin while the two side fins are asymmetrically foiled with the flat side on the inside. They will both point slightly inward towards the nose of the board.

Handle

The handles of the paddleboards have come a long away. Our very first paddleboards did not even have handles. The placement of the handle varies depending on the board. Some handles are placed slightly off centered to facilitate arm reach.

When choosing a board, make sure you are happy with the handle because you never know how far and for how long you will have to carry the board.

Air Vent

Not all boards have air vents; it depends on the material the paddleboard is built with. Most EPS boards have vents to allow for the expansion and contraction of the core material of the board due to changes in heat and atmospheric pressure. Make sure you know whether your board has one and know how to use it. If it has one, it is typically covered with a stainless steel screw-like plug or Goretex-like self-regulated plug.

Even the ones that are called self-regulated or hassle-free are not. You still need to make sure they stay clean and do not become clogged due to sand or salt residue, etc. We have found this out through many years and thousands of boards.

Paddle Board Construction 101

As of the writing of this book, there are 2 main types of boards: "Hard Boards" and "Inflatables". The terms are self-descriptive. Hard boards do not need a pump; inflatable boards require some sort of a pump.

Hard Boards - Basic Types

Hard boards typically have a core that is "hollow" or "solid".

Hollow boards come, in general, in 3 different types:

- Very heavy (in the order of 40 – 50 lbs for a 10' board), made of some type of plastic or plastic-like material.

- Very light (in the order of 18 – 24 lbs for a 12'6" board) made of high-end ultra-light material.

- Made of balsa wood or other type of sustainably grown wood.

Solid boards come, in general, with a styrene-based foam core or polyurethane based foam of one of the following types:

- EPS (Expanded Polystyrene, beaded foam core that will absorb water, the majority of the boards have vent screws).

- XTR (Extruded Polystyrene foam core, heavier, non-water absorbent foam).

- PU foam core (Polyurethane foam, heavier than EPS foam, is the traditional foam core surfboard construction method in use since the 1960's, generally less durable than EPS Epoxy boards.)

Hard Boards – Basic Construction

Most hard boards, these days, are made of polystyrene foam core and put together with an Epoxy formulation. Every epoxy formulation has its own specific mixing ratio of resin to hardener. This means that not all Epoxy boards are created equal.

Every board has (or should have) some type of reinforcement such as fiberglass, or Carbon, or Kevlar®, or combinations thereof. All these reinforcements come in a variety of arrangements, from random chopped-strand-mat, to woven cloths, to unidirectional tows. Some combine different raw materials, to tailor the composite to best handle particular loads.

To improve panel stiffness (decrease heel denting and such) most boards these days have some sort of sandwich structure. This consists of either of the following:

- Linear PVC foam (Airex)
- Cross-linked PVC foam (Divinycell)
- Wood veneer inserts.
- A combination of the above.

Also, where major local loads need to be accommodated, all boards have (or should have) inserts surrounding the fixtures. These inserts are commonly made from Divinycell (better for fin inserts) or high-density Urethane foam (less elastic).

The finish is typically one of the following:

- Resin (most commonly a Polyester finish resin - beautiful gloss but chips easily)
- Paint (Epoxy paints are most common in production boards, while customs usually have Linear Polyurethane paints - tough and long-lasting)
- ASA plastic skin (heavy and not particularly attractive, but takes major abuse gracefully)
- EVA foam padding (aka soft-top, common in rental boards)

Hard Boards – Basic TLC

Treat your hard board with tender, love and care, so that the water stays on the outside of your board!

"Water inside an EPS board due to injury or forgotten open vent will cause damage. Even the highest quality repair, will lead to permanent weight gain, as well as permanent propensity to suffer heat-related damage."

Tip – Keep It Cool!

Most materials change their molecular structure when heated dramatically. And so does the EPS foam in Epoxy boards. As it changes, it releases prodigious amounts of gas. That gas has to go somewhere. It will make itself room. It will blow a bubble.

So keep it cool! If you are comfortable, so is your board. If you feel sick from heat, so does your board. If you leave your board in a dark car, windows up, and the outside temperature is 95 degrees, the inside of your car may well go above 130 degrees.

- EPS foam outgasses at 130 degrees.
- Divinycell shrinks markedly at 130 degrees.
- Room-temperature-cure Epoxy resins turn brittle at 130 degrees.

The result at minimum is a reduced lifespan of your board. You may get away with a printing through of the reinforcements and inserts. But you may well end up with a bubble.

Tip – Keep It Clean & Dry!

If you are using a board bag for your hard board, never put it away wet and zip up the bag. The moisture that is attached to the board itself, will create water vapor in the bag when exposed to higher temperatures (substantial in a closed, dark car!). This water vapor can penetrate into paints, causing blisters.

Also, you do not want to be putting it in the board bag sandy, since over time the bag will turn into sand paper like material rubbing against your board.

Tip – Keep It Fresh!

If your board has vent plug, open it whenever you are off the water. It is the single most effective thing you can do to prolong the life of your board. Leaving it closed will cause the EPS foam core to expand and contract at least once a day. Over time, this will lead into board fatigue and possibly core weakness and failure. Remember to put it back on, BEFORE you hit the water.

Inflatable Paddle Boards

Inflatable SUPs feature an air core that is the result of durable waterproof PVC exterior with an internal webbing of drop-stitch construction. Thousands of fine polyester threads connect both the top and bottom layers, creating a stronger link that can withstand much higher pressures.

Inflatable paddle boards are great for:

- Fitness
- Yoga
- Running white water rivers
- People with limited storage
- Travel (whether car, air, etc.) Deflated, an iSUP fits into a large duffle type carry bag for transport and inflated it can be strapped on your car top like a hard board.

Here are some of the ISUP basic facts that you need to know.

- ISUP's typically come with a hand pump, a pressure gauge and a backpack for transporting the board.

- As of right now, they can be inflated to about 15-20 PSI producing a surprisingly rigid platform.

-   Some companies, these days, use an acrylic stiffening agent integrated in the deck, to improve stiffness and performance without adding weight or making the board harder to roll up.

-   Inflatable paddle boards often have webbing handles in the center of the board for easy carrying. Some boards also have webbing handles up front and on the tail to help you hold onto the board during a swim.

-   A really convenient feature exclusive to inflatable paddle boards is patches with stainless D-rings. They give you lots of options for attaching gear using bungee lacing. A lot of boards have already pre-attached such patches but you can also purchase them separately and glue them on yourselves.

-   The fins can be permanent (typically the side fins) or attached with a screw and a nut or quick release.

- As of right now, there are 2 main different types of pumps:

  - o Hand Pumps.
  - o Electric pumps that attaching to the car battery and/or a wall outlet for battery backup.

The pump technology continues to improve as we speak.

Inflatable Boards – Basic TLC

Inflatable boards do not require as much TLC as hard boards!

Tip – Do not leave it fully inflated when you are not using it

One of the most sensitive areas of an inflatable paddleboard is the seam area. If you typically inflate your board to 15 PSI while using it on the water or transporting it on the roof rack of your car, when not using, it deflate it to about 7 psi. Your board will last you a lot longer. Be careful to not over-inflate your board, follow the manufacturer's specifications and stay at least 1-2 PSI below the limit.

Tip – Do not inflate it with a pump of unknown origin

It may seem convenient and like a good idea to go to a gas station or use a tire pump or a bike pump but in the long run it will destroy your board. Use a pump that is designed exclusively for inflatable paddle board(s).

Tip – Protect the valve area

The valve is a very sensitive area of the board. Sand, salt, water, etc. can get in there and really mess up the air flow. When you are not inflating or deflating the board, make sure the valve is covered up.

Tip – Do not store it rolled up too tight and/or wet for long periods

Very often, it is inevitable to not have to roll up you board wet and put it in its backpack right after using it, for transportation purposes. But when you get back home or to your destination, unroll it, (clean it if possible with fresh water) and let it air dry. Afterwards, roll it up, put it in its backpack and loosen it up so it's not rolled tight. The seams will last longer.

Paddle Board Specifications 101

There are certain parameters that define the paddleboard and must be provided by the manufacturer. If the manufacturer cannot provide these parameters, look into a different brand.

Width

The distance measuring the widest area of your board from rail to rail.

Length

The distance measuring the longest area of your board from nose to tail.

Thickness

The distance measuring the thickest area of your board from the deck to the bottom across the rails.

Weight

The weight of your board.

Volume

The volume of the board is typically measured in liters and it is an indication of the buoyancy or flotation of the board. In other words, given the volume of the board you can calculate the maximum weight of a paddler of a given skill that it will support.

The dimensions of the board do not define the volume of the board. The volume of the board should be given to you by the manufacturer based on its design and construction.

In 2009, Pro-Surfer Whitney Guild, submerging boards in calibrated volume water tanks, was able to **create a volumetric table system named the "Guild Factor."**

Based on the Guild Factor for paddleboards, the volume of the board relates to the weight and the ability of the paddler as follows:

- Novice Paddler

  If you take the Volume of the board in liters, say V, and you multiply it by 1.1 then you get the Maximum Weight of a Novice paddler (in pounds) that it will support:

  V * 1.1 = Maximum Weight of a Novice paddler in pounds

- Intermediate Paddler

If you take the Volume of the board in liters, say V, and you multiply it by 1.3 then you get the Maximum Weight of an Intermediate paddler (in pounds) that it will support:

V * 1.3 = Maximum Weight of an Intermediate paddler in pounds

- Advanced Paddler

If you take the Volume of the board in liters, say V, and you multiply it by 1.7 then you get the Maximum Weight of an Advanced paddler (in pounds) that it will support.

V * 1.7 = Maximum Weight of an Advanced paddler in pounds

Through the years and thousands of clients, we have found this equation to be very accurate.

Thank you Whitney Guild!

Knowing your skill level, your weight, and the volume of the board you should be able to decide whether it will support you comfortably or not.

Chapter 2 – Your Paddle

Paddle Terminology 101

- **Paddle Handle** – The tallest part of the paddle where the raised arm grips the paddle at.
- **Paddle Shaft**– The shaft is the long part of the paddle that connects the handle down to the blade.
- **Paddle Throat** –The throat is the area of the paddle where the shaft and blade meet.
- **Paddle Blade** – The blade is the part that goes into the water to propel the paddleboard during a forward stroke.
- **Paddle Rails** – The angle at which the blade goes from the shaft to the widest part of the paddle including the widest part of the blade.
- **Paddle Face** – The side of the blade that faces the paddler.
- **Paddle Shaft Adjuster** –This is a feature exclusive to adjustable paddles.

Paddle Architecture 101

Paddle Shaft & Handle

As of right now, there are 3 main types of stand up paddles:

- Cut-to-Fit (the paddle comes in one solid piece and it is cu
-
- t to fit your size)
- Adjustable 2-piece (the paddle comes in two solid pieces and it can be adjusted to fit various paddler sizes and preferences)
- Adjustable 3-piece (aka Travel Paddles, self-explanatory)

The paddle shaft can be stiff or flex, depending on the material. The amount of flex defines the distribution of the energy from your body to the blade and vice a versa.

The shape of the shaft can be round, tapered round to oval, oval etc. depending on the design.

The material can be anywhere from aluminum, to fiberglass, wood, carbon fiber, polymer fiber, or a combination of the above, etc.

The paddle adjuster can be such as a pin and hole system, clamp, lever lock adjustable grip system, internal easy glide-twist to lock design, etc.

The paddle handle is often of some sort of ergonomic T-grip or palm grip.

Paddle Blade

The paddle blade can be made of plastic, wood, carbon fiber, fiberglass, lightweight PVC core, ABS reinforced rails, or a combination of the above, etc.

The face of the blade that pulls through the water during the power phase of a forward stroke, is often contoured to be concave to grab and hold as much water through the stroke as possible.

The angle of the paddle blade though the water and the blade's size affect the overall power and efficiency of your stroke. A well-balanced paddle blade squanders little energy; minimizing drag and maximizing power transfer throughout the stroke.

What you need to keep in mind when choosing a paddle

- Get a paddle that floats. Not all paddles float.

- Make sure you are happy with the size, shape and feel of the handle and shaft and the weight of the paddle.

- A cut-to-fit paddle is not your best option as your first paddle, unless you are positive that is the height of the paddle you are comfortable with.

- A wood paddle provides flex that takes pressure off the shoulders.

- 3-piece paddles are the inflatable paddleboard's best friend. They travel real well together. Do your homework though. Not all 3-piece paddles are created equal. A lot of 3-piece paddles have been known to break easily.

- Aluminum paddles may be very inexpensive but they tend to be heavy and become cumbersome after a while.

- Your height and weight alone do not necessarily determine the size of your paddle blade. The size of the paddle blade also highly depends on what style of paddling you enjoy.

- The smaller the blade, the less energy each stroke consumes and the less forward motion is generated.

- The bigger the blade, the more energy will be used and the more forward motion will be generated.

- If you enjoy a high cadence stroke, you will most likely enjoy a smaller blade size.

It's Your Paddle - Basic TLC

There are a couple of very easy things you can do that will help prolong the life of your paddle.

- Any time you set your paddle on your board lengthwise or on the ground, make sure that the throat of the paddle is in contact with the board or the ground. This way, you are reducing the chances of the throat snapping if for any reason weight is applied to it.

- When storing or transporting your paddle get in the habit of using a paddle bag or at least a paddle blade cover.

- After you are done using your paddle for the day, rinse your paddle with fresh water. If you have a 2-piece adjustable or a 3-piece paddle, take it apart and rinse it real well at all the connection points.

Chapter 3 - Safety Gear, Etc.

Leash

As you can probably tell by now, we believe that personal preference is highly relevant and important when it comes to attaining the utmost enjoyment while on the water.

Having said that, we also believe that wearing the proper leash is not a matter of personal preference. You should never go out paddling without wearing the proper leash for your area.

Wearing a leash could, have prevented most of the recorded paddleboard fatalities to this date that we are aware of. The proper leash is what keeps you attached to your board.

If you fall off the board, and you are not attached to it, chances are that you are going to have to swim after your board to catch it. Depending on several factors, you may not be able to catch your board. The consequences may be severe.

Also, during water rescues, it is a lot easier to spot a board on the water than a bobbing head.

Nowadays, there are different types of leashes available depending on the waterways. Most of the leashes come as either straight or coiled and there are even hybrids.

Do not confuse straight leashes with surfboard leashes. Most surfboard leashes will snap due to the paddleboard weight. This was our only option back when we first started paddle boarding, so we know first hand.

Paddleboard leashes can be attached to your ankle, calf, or waist, again, depending on the waterway.

For flat water, we have found that coiled calf leashes work the best. They do not get caught in seaweed and other obstacles in the water and at the same time they stay off the deck of the board.

As always, decide based on your own water circumstances and make sure you have access to some form of quick release mechanism, in case you need to get separated from your board for safety reasons.

Life Jacket/Whistle

The U.S. Coast Guard classifies stand up paddleboards as vessels, therefore, whenever you are paddling navigational waterways, you have to have one of the following three:

- An easily accessible inherently buoyant Personal Floatation Device and whistle on your board.
- An inherently buoyant Personal Floatation Device and easily accessible whistle on your person.
- A "waist" life jacket and easily accessible whistle on your person.

We always recommend that it is best to wear a life jacket / whistle.

Towing System

We believe that every one, when out on the water, should be prepared and ready to tow another board in order to assist a fellow paddle boarder.

We always carry the following 3 pieces:

- 10'-15' rope in the form of a rock climbing rabbit ear sling
- Paddle Carabiner
- 3-In-1 sea sucker vacuum mount

This system is also handy if for some reason you need to temporarily keep your paddle out of the way.

Carabiner

A load bearing stainless steel carabiner is always handy in terms of safety.

Dry Bag

We like to use the dry bag for the first aid kit and the cell phone in case of emergency. Ziploc style bags are not dry bags.

Rock Climbing Sling

We like to wear it over our shoulder and across the chest and attach the dry bag with the stainless steel carabiner for faster access to everything.

They are typically measured in centimeters. A 60cm (approximately 24") should work just right.

Knife or Leatherman Wave

- Any time rope is involved, entanglement may occur.

Waterproof Watch

Wearing a watch allows you to keep track of time so much easier than having to check the phone.

Puka Patch – Or a high end sticker

This is only applicable if you are on a hard board. If for some reason, you ding your board and you are on the water, this will prevent your board from absorbing more water until you are in a position to take your board off the water.

Cargo Area

It is always nice to have some sort of deck cargo storage area for things such as your water bottle, dry bag, etc. A lot of boards come with it but a lot of them do not.

If your board does not come with it, here are your options:

On a hard board:

- You can use suction cup deck rigging kit.
- Do not glue on your board.
- Do not drill into your board.
- Any permanent alterations to your board will weaken it.
- If the suction cups do not adhere to the hard board and the hard board has no attachments whatsoever to run bungee cords through, do not purchase that board.

On an inflatable board:

- You can glue D-ring patches and run bungee cords through them.
- Make sure you use the appropriate material D-ring patch and glue.
- Gluing the correct type of patch using the correct glue strengthens your board.

Shoes

It is of the utmost importance that you protect your feet while stand up paddling on flat water. You never know what you might step on that could take you out of commission, anywhere from a couple of hours to a few days (barnacles, fishing hooks, broken glass, stingrays, etc.)

Having said that, you want shoes that will still allow your feet to be solid on the board. In other words you want as little cushion as possible in between the feet and the deck for maximum grip. This is what the minimalist amphibious style of shoes is designed for.

We use the Five-Finger ones. Through many years of water and other activities, we have tried every possible type of shoe and these are the ones that work best for us for flat-water paddling.

Clothing

Any time you are out on the board, prepare for immersion. This means:

- Wear clothes that you are comfortable swimming in.
- Wear clothes that are not too hot or uncomfortable while on your board.

Here is what we have found through our experience

- Wetsuits are only good if you are planning on paddle surfing and spending a lot of time in the water. If you are going to stay on your board and out of the water, a wet suit becomes bulky, heavy, restrictive and hot.

- In cooler weather, we like to use a wetsuit – like material instead, it is called Hydroskin. It gives you the right amount of warmth without the bulky or restrictive feeling.

- Do not use cotton, or blue jeans, they get heavy and they can drag you underwater.

When it comes to safety, as a rule of thumb:

- Know your area.
- Think about the worse conditions you are likely to encounter.
- Carry the necessary safety gear that will help you deal with them successfully.
- You want gear that is robust, simple to use and can serve multiple purposes.
- Know your gear.

PART II

Chapter 4

Kneeling Paddle Techniques

It is an undeniable fact that every one learns differently. What has worked for you may not work for others. Keep an open mind, look for what might resonate best for every person and keep things simple. Einstein said that "if you can't explain it to a six year old, you don't understand it yourself."

What we are going to give you here, is the simplest way to get some one new on the board and have them standing and enjoying, in almost no time. We have had to improvise anywhere from asking people to stand on benches (to practice paddle strokes) to attaching a 35' rope to the back of their board, let them paddle out, tow them back in and repeat until they mastered the technique.

We like to use an inflatable paddleboard on the sand or on the grass (without any fins attached) as a learning and demonstration platform. By having some one stand on an unfamiliar object (the paddleboard) and experience what it feels like while in a controlled environment (on land) as opposed to an uncontrolled environment (on the water) you take away a significant part of their fear.

Here we go!

Step 1 – Get a feel for the board

Keep your shoes on until you get on the board. You never know when you might step on something unpleasant that might even cut the bottom of your foot.

Now, take your shoes off and get on the board (on land).

- Come standing approximately in the middle of the board, around the handle area.
- Face the nose of the board.
- Stand with your feet a little further than hip distance apart and the toes pointing forward.

- Bounce up and down a couple of times and see how stable the board feels.

- This is the point where pretty much every one feels like a little kid.

Step 2 – Hold your paddle, kneeling

Now go on your knees and stand on your knees, do not sit on your heels. You are approximately in the middle of the board, around the handle area facing the nose of the board.

Hold the paddle with your hands as far apart on the shaft as comfortable. This gives you a lot more leverage.

For the sake of simplicity, let's assume that your left hand is the low hold and your right hand the high hold. The left hand should be an overhand grip and the right hand an underhand grip.

Step 3 – Paddle forward, kneeling

This is the most fundamental paddling stroke that you need to master first.

- Without leaning forward, extend your arms fully, reaching as far forward as comfortable. Your raised hand should be at approximately nose to forehead level.

  - Put the full blade of your paddle vertically in the water, close to the left rail of your board, almost scraping it (but not really).

  - It is important that you put the whole blade in the water, all the way to the throat but no further. This gives you a lot more power.

- Engaging your glutes and the rest of your core, pretend that you are pulling your body towards your paddle and keeping your blade in the water bring it to about your knees. This propels your board forward.

- Once there, retrieve the blade by slicing it through the water, away from the board (i.e. lowering your right arm and bringing the paddle shaft closer to the board.)

  - Do not attempt to take the blade out of the water by lifting the shaft higher, you would be causing unnecessary strain to your shoulder and negatively affecting the speed/direction of your board.

  - Make sure the blade is all the way out of the water before you start setting up for the next paddle stroke.

- The next paddle stroke can be on the same side (along the left rail) or on the opposite (along the right rail.) There are no rules in terms of the number of strokes that should be performed on each side. You do what it takes to get you to where you are heading making the most efficient use of the wind, current and all other environmental components.

- In order to switch paddling sides, the top (right) hand slides down, staying in contact with the shaft the whole time, as the blade moves over to the other side. The right hand has now automatically become an overhand grip and as the left hand shifts to the top it becomes an underhand grip.

Step 4 – Backpaddle, kneeling

This is the second most important paddle stroke. You will need this any time you need to make a turn or stop.

For the sake of simplicity, let's assume that you want to turn left.

- Hold your paddle with your left hand in the low overhand grip and your right hand in the high underhand grip. So the paddle is on the left side of the board.

- Put the blade in the water, as far back towards the tail as you can reach, comfortably. The power face of the paddle is facing the tail of your board.

- Keep the blade vertical and close to your board (as if you were scraping the rail but not really) and pretending that you are pulling your body towards your paddle bring it to about your knees. This turns your board left.

- Once there, retrieve the blade by slicing it through the water, away from the board(i.e. lowering your right arm and bringing the paddle shaft closer to the board.)

  o Make sure the blade is all the way out of the water before you start setting up for the next paddle stroke.

- If you do this right:

  o You should not need more than 2 reverse strokes and 1 forward stroke on the opposite side to turn towards any direction you wish.

- ○ You should be able to stop with as few as 2 reverse strokes (1 on each side.)

Step 5 – Draw stroke, kneeling

Draw strokes are used to move your board sideways so you can pull close to a dock or another board.

For the sake of simplicity, let's assume that your target is on the left side of you.

- Hold your paddle so that your left hand is the low hold and your right hand the high hold. The left hand should be an overhand grip and the right hand an underhand grip.

- Look at your target and extend your arms as far towards your target as comfortable with the face of the blade facing your left rail.

- Put the blade fully in the water, keep looking at your target and pretending that you are pulling your body towards your paddle bring it to about your knees.

- To retrieve, twist the blade 90° so the blade can slice (feather) through the water away from the board.

    - Do not allow the blade to get sucked under your board, this could cause your board to tip.

- Repeat as many draw strokes as needed.

Chapter 5 – Falling

What we have discovered, over the past few years is that even though every one learns differently, there is a fundamental concern, common to most first time paddlers: The fear of falling.

Falling

There is actually a way to properly fall to help decrease the chances of something "bad" happening. With a little bit of practice, you can even learn to enjoy it as well!

How to properly fall

- If you are on a hard board, it is very important that you fall off the board and in the water. Falling on a hard board, the board can hurt you, causing you to experience anywhere from a simple bruise to a broken nose, etc. It is also possible that you can damage the board. Though fixable, it might take your board out of commission for a few weeks and your hard board will never be the same.

- As you are about to fall, do not hesitate, do not try and save yourself from falling. You can even use your feet to push the board away from you.

- Fall with your butt going in the water first, with your legs bent. This way, you minimize the chances of spraining an ankle on the bottom.Do not fall with your head first.

- A good way to fall is to go straight off the back of the board. Never jump in front of the board, or you will risk it hitting you in the head.

- Keep your paddle in your hand but away from your face.

- Know what is on the bottom, so if you are on a shallow area you don't push off anything that can hurt you. Also, whether you fall or jump off the board, do it expecting shallow water, two or three feet below you, to protect yourself. If you expect it to be deeper and it is not, you can hurt yourself.

- Once in the water, know where your board is. You don't want the water pushing a hard board on you. You may need to use your hands to protect your head.

- Stay calm, panicking only makes things worse by wasting your energy. Relax, enjoy the water, pull your board closer to you by pulling on your leash, survey the situation and stay away from any obstacles.

How to get back up on the board

Place your paddle on the board, parallel to the board so that the blade is towards the nose and the handle towards the tail, with the face of the paddle down, i.e. the tip of the blade is pointing up, away from the deck. This way, you minimize the risk of breaking your paddle.

Bring both arms on the board, and keeping your paddle secure in between the deck of the board and your arms, reach (width-wise) as far across on the board as you can towards the opposite rail.

Keep your board leveled with the water by applying vertical pressure on it with your arms and your upper body, otherwise there is the risk of your board tipping over due to your weight.

Depending on how wide your board is and on the length of your arms, you may need to maneuver slightly towards the nose or towards the tail for further reach.

Push the board onto the water with your arms and using as much strength as you have crawl onto your board sliding one leg up at a time so that you end up in the prone position on your board, facing the nose.

Once you have gotten on your board and you are safe, stay seated or on your knees and take a second to catch your breath. Think about what you did well and what you can improve on. Recall how it felt so next time you are in the water, you can think back to this moment and remember that even if it feels scary, you will eventually be back up on your board.

Survey the situation and paddle away from any obstacles.

Chapter 6

Paddle Standing - How Sweet It Is...

How to adjust the length of your paddle

It is always best to set up your paddle height on land. You can always fine-tune it later while on your board and on the water.

- Stand barefoot, on an even ground so that your feet and bottom tip of the paddle blade are on the same level.
- Reach up with one arm and grab the handle of the paddle, not just the shaft.
- You want your raised arm extended with a very slight bend on your elbow.
- If in doubt, it is safer to go higher rather than lower.
- That is the ideal paddle length for you for recreational and SUP & Yoga paddling.

How to get on your board

- The board needs to be on the water.
- Put on your leash and make sure it is properly attached to your board.

- Get on your board on your knees, in your tabletop pose, knees underneath hips, hands underneath shoulders.
- Position your upper body approximately above the handle of your board.
- Set your paddle on your board, perpendicular to your board and hold it with both hands, keeping your fingers on your board. So, basically you are securing your paddle in between your hands and your board.
- Bring one foot forward, almost in between your hands.
- Bring, the other foot forward, in line with the first foot.
- Keeping your knees bent, and your stomach tight, grab your paddle, stand up and immediately stick your paddle blade in the water.
- If you get all excited and just stand there and start looking all around you, chances are you are going to fall in the water. □
- If you fall, please, fall in the water, not on your board, especially, if you are using a hard board, as opposed to inflatable. Inflatable boards are a lot more forgiving than hard boards. Hard boards can hurt you, anywhere from a knee bruise to a broken nose, etc.

How to hold your paddle during a Forward Stroke

- One hand needs to be holding the handle of the paddle and the other hand needs to be as far down as possible, while comfortable, for leverage.
- You should be facing the face of the paddle so that the "scoop" of the paddle at the paddle throat is facing away from you. You do not want to be "scooping" the water, as counter-intuitive as this might seem. Your goal is to propel your board through the water, by pulling your body towards your paddle.
- Your grip should be soft. This applies for both hands. You should be barely using your fingers. During all phases of your paddle stroke, the finger hold should be so gentle that if you were to stop paddling, your paddle would slide out of your hands.
- Your arms should be as straight as possible, in other words, your elbows should feel almost locked. This will assist you in using a lot more of your core strength as opposed to your extremities (arms and legs).
- If you feel you look odd while paddling, like a robot, you are probably doing it right.

The Forward Stroke

We are now ready to precisely define our Forward Stroke. We have done all the groundwork in the kneeling chapter and in the "how to hold you paddle during a forward stroke" above.

Our Forward Stroke consists of 4 parts that seamlessly follow one another.

Extend/Reach → Push → Pull → Retrieve

- Without leaning forward, extend your arms fully, reaching as far forward as comfortable.

- With your top hand on the paddle handle, push so that the whole blade of your paddle goes vertically in the water.

- With your bottom hand, pull your body towards your paddle and keeping your blade in the water bring it to about your knees.

- Once there, retrieve the blade by slicing it through the water, away from the board.

Backpaddle Standing

- The only difference from the kneeling position is that the top hand has to be on the handle of the paddle.

Draw Stroke Standing

- The only difference from the kneeling position is that the top hand has to be on the handle of the paddle.

The Sweet Spot

The sweet spot is the area of your paddleboard where you are the most balanced while standing.

What that means is that

- You feel stable standing
- The nose and the tail of your board are not sinking in the water.
- The rails are even.

The location of this area is typically surrounding the center of mass of your board but its dimensions depend on the architecture and construction of your board. Typically, the handle of the paddleboard is within the Sweet Spot of the board.

In general, paddle boards made for surfing have a very small sweet spot and paddle boards made for yoga / fitness have a very large sweet spot.

The quickest way to start becoming familiar with a board you have not used before is to find its Sweet Spot.

How to find the Sweet Spot of your board

Once you are standing comfortably on your board, walk a few inches forward until the nose of the board starts sinking. Then start walking back until the tail of the board starts sinking.

You have found the space in between the nose and the tail, where neither the nose nor the tail is sinking. That is the length of the Sweet Spot of your board.

Standing within that area, keeping your feet at a

comfortable distance (at least hip distance) start shifting them to either side of the board, i.e. towards the rails. Notice how far your can go without the rails becoming uneven. You have found the space in between the rails that defines the width of the Sweet Spot of your board.

Yin Paddling

Our philosophy in life is based on two fundamental principles:

- Economy of action.
- Smart play.

"Economy of action" is the term we use to describe the ability to accomplish as much as possible with as little effort as possible. In other words, it is the ability to generate minimal waste.

"Smart play" is the term we use to describe the ability to perform any physical activity, indoors or outdoors long-term without injury. In other words, it is the ability to wear out (playing), not rust out (from injury.)

We also believe that the way you do anything is the way you do everything. So we always look for the most economically efficient and the smartest (long-term) technique in any physical activity. Having applied this to paddle boarding, we developed the Yin Paddling Technique.

The mechanical foundation of the Yin Paddling is described above in the "How to hold your paddle during a forward stroke" section.

- Your arms should be as straight as possible, in other words, your elbows should feel almost locked.

- If you feel you look odd while paddling, like a robot, you are probably doing it right.

The goal of the Yin Paddling is to use as much of your fascia, your Yin type of tissue (connective tissue) as possible and as little of your muscle tissue as possible.

Benefits of Yin Paddling Include

- More sustained power to your strokes.
- Less wear and tear on your joints (hips, low back, knees, etc.)
- Less typical muscle activation, so longer lasting muscle use, hence longer paddling time.
- Increased joint mobility leading to performance increase in other sports (cross-training.)
- Deeper breathing due to thoracic diaphragm activation.

For another perspective on Yin Paddling, you may wish to read:

Popular Mechanics: The Science Of Bruce Lee's One Inch Punch

Mark's Daily Apple Blog:
http://www.marksdailyapple.com/why-i-paddle-board-and-why-you-should-try-it/#axzz3xniQ0mU9

PART III

Chapter 7

Safety Tips

There are numerous things that you can do to make your time on the water safer but these are the "obvious" (as in common sense) things that you should always consider.

- You should always wear a life-jacket, or at least have one on your board. Remember, your board floats on its own; it does not need a life jacket attached to it. :-) It is federal law that any one outside the surf zone must have a life jacket and whistle with them.

- Wear a proper (for stand up paddling in your area) leash with a quick release mechanism that attaches you to your board.

- If a safety issue does occur stay with you board. It is easier to see a board floating on the water than a person. If it is more dangerous to stay with your board than not to stay with your board, then, please, do not stay with your board. Remember to use your common sense. :-)

- Have a float plan in place with a responsible adult. Some one should always know where you are going and what time you are supposed to be back. They should also know what to do if you do not return.

- Know your waters. Whether you are paddling on the ocean, on a river or on a lake you need to know if there are any safety risks related to the area.

- Know your weather. There is no bad weather, there is wrong gear. And sometimes the paddle board is the wrong gear. There are just certain times that you should not be going out.

- Do your hard paddle first. Paddle out into the wind or into the current first when you have the strength and energy. That way, you can rest more on the way back in.

- Wear your cell phone in a dry bag that is attached to you.

- Take a safety class by qualified instructors who care.

- Always paddle with a pal. Try to find a stand up paddle club in your area. If there isn't one, create one!

Chapter 8

Towing & Rescue

Our experience has taught us that when it comes to safety, three principles are key:

- Prevention – Do not wait until something "bad" happens before you do something about it.

- Simplicity – Whatever your technique is, keep it as simple as possible, every second counts, complexity can be fatal.

- Efficiency – Your gear and your skills need to be as efficient as possible, minimize your overhead, and make your actions as economical as possible.

Based on these three principles, we are presenting three techniques that address every possible situation you are going to encounter during flat-water stand up paddling:

- Towing

- Easy Rescue

- Unconscious Victim Rescue

We designed, streamlined and perfected these techniques over the years, having taken thousands of people of all skills and abilities out on the water.

We invite you to practice these "drills" regularly so they become second nature to you.

Towing

There are several tow setups you can do (such as inline tow, V-tow, husky tow) depending on the number of guides and/or experienced paddlers in your group.

We are only analyzing the simplest type of towing here, which is the single tow.

Single Tow

The single tow involves 2 boards, yours and the "victim's." Be prepared to tow, any time you get on the water. Remember, this simple habit could save some one's life.

When to use

Risk Assessment and Safety Management is addressed in the following chapter. However, you always, need to use your own judgment and assess the situation.

As a rule of thumb, if the victim is unconscious or unable to stay safely on their own board, do not use the single tow.

Equipment

The equipment that you need is what was listed under "Towing System" in Chapter 3.

- 10'-15' rope in the form of a rock climbing rabbit ear sling
- Paddle Carabiner
- 3-In-1 sea sucker vacuum mount

How To Perform

There are 3 major steps to towing:

- Setting Up Your Towing System
- Attaching Your Towing System To The "Victim's" Board
- Paddling to Safety

You can perform the single tow in 2 different ways, depending on where you attach your end of the rope:

- To your board
- To your person

Single Tow Attaching To Your Board

Set Up Your Towing System

1. Run the sling through a tail attachment on your board and insert one end of it (ear) through the other end (ear).

The tail attachment on your board should be one of the following:

   a. On an inflatable board a D-ring, typically on the deck or underneath. Most inflatable boards have D-ring attachments towards the nose. If it doesn't and you have control over the board, all you have to do is buy one and glue it on. Make sure you get the type of material that will work for your board.

b. On an "epoxy finish" hard board, a sea-sucker that you attach on the deck, towards the tail.

c. On a plastic finish hard board, the handle that these boards typically have.

d. If none of the above is an option, you will need to follow the steps of "Single Tow Using Your Person"

2. Hook the paddle carabiner to the free ear (the ear not at the tail). Check that the carabiner is secure.

3. Secure the sea sucker vacuum mount to the carabiner.

4. Attach the carabiner, somewhere out of the way, on a bungee cord towards the nose of your board.

You are now ready!

Attach Your Towing System To The "Victim's" Board

1. Paddle as fast as you can, safely, towards the "victim", asking them to stay calm, relax and just "hang out".

2. Once you are a couple of feet away from them, follow one of the two options:

    - Ask them to sit on their board, hand them the blade of your paddle, ask them to hold onto it firmly and pull your board towards theirs.

    If they are not able to stay seated and/or grab and hold your paddle blade, pull up towards their board as fast as you canand safely, use their board to stop you (do not allow hard board to hard board hit).

3. Your board is now rail to rail next to their board. It does not matter if the two boards are facing the same way or opposite ways.

4. Slide your board forward or back so that you have easy access to their board's nose.

5. Unattach your carabiner from Step 5 in the "Set Up" section above and perform one of the following depending on the "victim's" board:

   a. If their board is an inflatable with a D-ring on the deck or underneath, attach only your carabiner to it and put the sea sucker vacuum mount away (on the board or on your person) since you do not need it in this case. Check that your carabiner is secure.

   b. If their board is a hard board of an "epoxy finish", first attach the sea sucker vacuum mount on their deck, close to the nose and next the carabiner to the sea sucker's ring. Check that both the sea sucker and the carabiner are secure. The sea sucker will work on most epoxy surface boards.

c. If their board is a hard board of a plastic finish, attach the carabiner to the handle that these boards typically have towards the nose. Check that the carabiner is secure.

d. If none of the above is an option, hand the end of the tow rope to the "victim", ask them to hold onto it until you tell them otherwise and put your carabiner and sea sucker vacuum mount away.

You are now attached!

Paddle to Safety

1. If the "victim" is able to safely use their paddle allow them to assist you.

2. Advise the "victim" to keep their arms and legs on their board for safety. Make sure they are safe and comfortable.

3. There are cases where you may need to take their paddle or any of their extra gear away and place it on your board, for safety.

4. Paddle any way you wish as long as it is safe for you and the "victim".

5. Remember that if you are paddling standing, it may be more challenging due to the pulling that you will be experiencing caused by the victim's board.

You can now paddle away to a safe location!

Single Tow Attaching To Your Person

Set Up Your Towing System

If you are wearing a Type V Rescue life jacket you have a quick-release rescue belt, with a stainless steel attachment ring. You always need a quick-release mechanism in case you need to detach your person from the rope for safety.

1. Run the sling through the stainless steel attachment ring, and insert one end of it (ear) through the other end (ear).

2. Hook the paddle carabiner to the free ear (the ear not attached to your life jacket.) Check that the carabiner is secure.

3. Secure the sea sucker vacuum mount to the carabiner.

4. Attach the carabiner, somewhere out of the way, using one of the hooks of your very functional life jacket.

You are now ready!

Attach Your Towing System To The "Victim's" Board

Follow the steps from the corresponding section in the "Single Tow Using Your Board" modifying Step 5 as follows:

"Unattach your carabiner from **Step 4** in the "Set Up" section above and perform one of the following depending on the "victim's" board:"

You are now attached!

Paddle to Safety

Follow the steps from the corresponding section in the "Single Tow Using Your Board".

You can now paddle away to a safe location!

Easy Rescue

You will need to use this technique any time the "victim" has fallen off their board and needs assistance getting back on. The Easy Rescue assumes that the "victim" is conscious and able to follow directions.

We developed this technique after noticing that the two most common issues people encounter after falling off their board are:

- Lack of strength and endurance to climb back up on the board (falling takes a lot of energy away.)

- The board "capsizing" during the process of them climbing up (due to their weight pushing down on one side.)

How To Perform

There are two different cases we need to consider:

- The "Victim" Has Hold Of Their Board
- The "Victim" Does Not Have Hold Of Their Board

The "Victim" Has Hold Of Their Board

If the "victim" has their leash on (as guides we make our clients wear leashes during our guided trips) they will have hold of their board and life is good!

1. Paddle as fast as you can, safely, towards the "victim", asking them to keep their arms on their board, stay calm, relax and just "hang out".

2. Approach their board from the side that they are not on, so you do not run into them.

3. Use their board to stop you (do not allow hard board to hard board hit).

4. Your board is now rail to rail next to their board. It does not matter if the two boards are facing the same way or opposite ways.

5. If you are not already on your knees, go on your knees.

6. Place your paddle horizontally across both boards so their board is wedged under your paddle and next to your board.

7. Put one hand on their board, pushing the board down, extend your other arm towards them and ask them to grab your forearm, hold onto it and pull themselves

up crawling on their board one leg at a time, ending up on their belly.

8. It is very important that not only do you stay solid on your board, you are also able to hold their board stable and flat on the water as well. This way you are creating an anchor point for them to be able to climb back up on their board.

9. They are now on their board lying on their belly. Make sure they are facing the nose of their board, so if they are not, ask them to turn.

10. Secure their paddle and the rest of their gear on their board and/or your board.

11. Assess the situation to decide if they need to be towed or they can continue to paddle by themselves and proceed accordingly.

The "Victim" Does Not Have Hold Of Their Board

Remember that when on the water, you are a guide first, a recreational paddler second.

The hierarchy of your priorities is as follows:

1. Rescue the person.
2. Retrieve their board.
3. Retrieve their paddle.
4. Retrieve the rest of their gear.

Assess the situation and decide whether the person can swim comfortably until you have retrieved their board or not. If there is any doubt regarding their well-being, you ignore the board and the rest of the gear and proceed following one of the two scenarios depending on the volume of your board:

Your Board Supports Two People

As guides, our boards always support 2 people.

1. Paddle as fast as you can, safely, towards the "victim", asking them to stay calm, relax and just "hang out".

2. As soon as you get a couple of feet away from them, get on your knees, hand them the blade of your paddle, ask them to hold firmly on it and pull them towards your board.

3. Turn to face them, extend one arm towards them, ask them to grab your forearm, hold onto it and pull themselves up crawling on the board one leg at a time, ending up on their belly.

4. They are now on your board, in front of you, lying on their belly. Ask them to make themselves confortable, staying on their belly or sitting, facing the nose of the board.

5. Stay behind them and paddle to safety.

Your Board Does Not Support Two People

If you are out on a recreational paddle with a board that only supports one person, you can still assist the "victim" until you get help.

1. Paddle as fast as you can, safely, towards the "victim", asking them to stay calm, relax and just "hang out".

2. As soon as you get a couple of feet away from them, get on your knees, hand them the blade of your paddle, ask them to hold firmly on it and pull them towards your board.

3. Ask them to put their arms on your board and rest.

4. Get off your board from the opposite side, set your paddle horizontally width-wise across the board with the blade towards your side and use your upper body to keep the board flat on the water.

5. Ask the "victim" to hold onto the paddle shaft firmly and pull themselves up crawling on the board one leg at a time, ending up on their belly.

6. They are now on your board lying on their belly. Ask them to make themselves comfortable, staying on their belly or sitting, facing the nose of the board.

7. Stay in the water, towards the tail holding onto the board and "swim" towards safety.

Unconscious "Victim" Rescue

This technique refers to when the "victim" has fallen off their board and is unconscious or not able to follow directions.

In this case, your only concern is to get the person to safety as quickly as possible. Their gear is no longer of a concern.

How To Perform

We recommend that you get specialized training, since there are too many factors that come into play.

Keep in Mind...

It is very important that you practice rescue skills regularly and continue to expand your repertoire.

No matter what environment you are paddling in and who your fellow paddlers are, always consider yourself a guide and act accordingly.

Never rush into any situation without quickly evaluating it first to choose the best course of action. You do not want to become a victim and make a bad situation worse by adding yourself into the "needs help" side of the equation.

Chapter 9

Guiding

Guide Board

A guide board is the type of paddle board that gives you all the features you need to comfortably and safely guide a trip and successfully respond to any towing or rescue need.

Through our experience, we have found that there are 6 main features that define a guide board:

- It can hold two people.
- It has good attachments for towing.
- It maneuvers easily.
- It is relatively fast.
- It is simple to use.
- It can easily store and carry safety gear.

All of the above bullets are self-explanatory based on the previous chapters of the book.

Guiding Principles

Float Plan

Any time you get on the water, whether alone or not, you must leave a float plan with some one who has common sense and you trust and who is not getting on the water with you for that trip.

The float plan includes but it is not limited to:

- The number of people in your group.

- The number of paddle boards and preferably colors of the boards also.

- Your car's color, make and license number (at both locations if the launching and landing areas are different.)
- The launching site.

- The route you will be taking.

- The expected landing site.

- The expected time of return.

- What the trusted person should do if they have not heard from you by a certain time such as contacting the Coast Guard, or Law Enforcement, or Fire Rescue, etc.

- The exact phone numbers of the agencies to contact in case of emergency.

- Optional: Description of group members, paddling ability, signaling devices, medical concerns and how well they are prepared in terms of rescue and shelter gear.

It is your responsibility to honor the float plan and notify the trusted person as soon as you are safely back on land.

Group Setup & Configuration

We have found that the optimal ratio for a safe and fun trip is at least 1 guide per 5 paddlers (5 paddlers not including the guide.) This means that with 6 – 10 paddlers we have a second guide and so on.

5 Paddlers or Less

The guide is leading, setting the pace, staying within talking distance with all the paddlers and making sure that no one is falling behind.

6 – 10 Paddlers

There is a guide as the lead and a guide as the last person in the group. No one is to pass the lead guide and the last person (the guide in the back) has to always be the last person. The last person needs to be the strongest paddler and guide in terms of ability and experience since they will be the ones tending to a towing or rescue need. Never let a paddler be last. The 2 guides can communicate with non-verbal signs.

11 – 15 Paddlers

There is a guide as the lead, a guide as the last person in the group and a guide "out to the side" creating a diamond configuration, using the shoreline as one of the points of the diamond. No one is to get outside of the third guide.The 3 guides can communicate with non-verbal signs.

16 – 20 Paddlers

A full diamond configuration will be created. All guides use radio communication.

21 Paddlers Or More

With more than 21 paddlers the extra guides paddle inside the diamond configuration assisting every one with paddling advice or simply making sure every paddler feels comfortable, safe and is having fun!

We have guided successfulpaddleshaving as many as 33 paddlers using these techniques.

Communication

When paddling in a group, to guarantee the safety of the group,it is highly important that:

- Every paddler is responsible for himself or herself.
- All paddlers are within communication range of each other.

The communication can be done in one of the following 3 ways:

- Verbal Communication
- Non – Verbal Communication – Arm Signaling
- Non – Verbal Communication – Whistle Signaling

It feels very rewarding to assist your fellow paddlers stay safe and have a great time by keeping them informed. Keep your eyes open for any obstacles or awesome wildlife scenery and point them out to the rest of your group as soon as you spot them.

Verbal Communication

It is the most reliable and preferred form of communication.

It can be direct, if all the paddlers are within talking distance or over the radio, in between the guides.

Non – Verbal Communication

With groups involving more than 5 people, you need to be prepared in case direct verbal communication is not an option for all the paddlers involved, due to unpredictable environmental circumstances.

Disclaimer: The Non – Verbal Communication Signals below are not international signals, we developed them using our kayaking and scuba diving background and we have found that they work very well for us and our clients. We will continue to use them until international signs are formulated and approved.

Non – Verbal Communication – Arm/Paddle Signaling

Before your trip begins, agree upon these simple arm/paddle signals that everyone can use to communicate basic messages:

1. Holding the paddle with the blade pointing:

    a. Up and at about a 45-degree angle to the right means – "Go right safely."
    b. Up and at about a 45-degree angle to the left means – "Go left safely."
    c. Straight up, vertically means – "Stop safely."

2. Holding the paddle with the blade pointing up and slowly creating a large circle means – "Gather around and/or come to me safely."

3. Holding the paddle with the blade pointing up and swinging the paddle quickly back and forth means – "Emergency/Danger."

4. Pointing at some one and then tapping the top of your head with your fist (thumb side down, pinky side up) means – "Are you ok?"

    The person that the "Are you ok?" signal was addressed to must respond in the same manner, otherwise, it means they are NOT ok and you must head towards them.

For all of the above signals, the guides must repeat the communication signal that was initiated so that the lead guide knows the signal has been seen by all guides.

Non – Verbal Communication – Whistle Signaling

This is another form of communication that again, you agree upon, before your trip begins.

One blast: "Attention – Come or look this way, safely."

Two blasts: "Stop – I need to stop or bring the group to a stop, safely."

Three blasts: "Emergency – A paddler is in trouble or we have a problem."

Reading The Weather

Always check the weather forecast before you launch and learn your area's weather patterns. For example, in our area, during the summer months, we schedule most of our trips for early to mid morning because if lightening hits it is typically in the afternoon.

These days, there are several good apps for the phone that give you the local weather with radar, tide graphs, NOAA Ocean Buoys, etc. Experiment with them so you can find the ones that work the best for your area, and use them to identify weather patterns.

If you will be paddling in a new area, foreign to you, ask the locals (trusted ones).

Also, never underestimate the power of good old sailor proverbs. Here are three of our favorite examples:

"Red sky at morning, sailor take warning; Red

sky at night, sailor's delight."

When you see a red sunset, you are observing the sun's rays through suspended dust particles. If the suspended dust is dry, the sunset will appear red; if it is wet, the sunset will appear as a yellow or gray orb that is seen through the haze.

Since most weather patterns move from west to east (especially storm systems), you are looking at tomorrow's weather.

So a red sky at sunset predicts fair, dry conditions for the following day. A red sunrise, on the other hand, is lighting up the cirrus or cirrostratus clouds that are moving into an area. These clouds are the beginning of a weather pattern leading to thicker and lower clouds that could well turn wet over the course of the day, or at best, remain unsettled.

"When a halo rings the moon and sun, the rain will come upon the run".

There are many proverbs that use the presence of a halo around the moon or sun to predict the weather. When you observe a halo, you are seeing the development of clouds at higher altitudes. The cirrus and cirrostratus clouds are part of the same weather pattern described above and predict wet or unsettled weather within 24 hours.

"Wind that swings around the sun, and winds that bring the rain are one; Winds that swing against the sun, keep the rain storm on the run."

If the wind is moving from east to west, like that of the sun, skies will usually be clear. These veering winds (clockwise) often follow a cold front as they clear the air and bring a rise in barometric pressure.

If the wind moves opposite the sun's path from west to east, wet or unsettled weather is generally in the offing. These backing (counterclockwise) winds usually are part of a warm from and a gradually falling barometer.

"A backing wind says storms are nigh (near); a veering wind will clear the sky."

Good Guiding Habits

- Dress for immersion, i.e. always assume you are going to get wet!
- Wear your PFD, whistle and leash.
- Have your towing system ready.

- Wear your watch, your phone in the dry bag and knife.
- Become familiar with the waterway you are paddling before taking clients out there.
- Check weather forecast and tide predictions before you launch.
- Use gear appropriate for the conditions and keep safety gear accessible.
- Do not take people out in weather/water that is rougher than the conditions you have trained in.
- Do not take new paddlers out for an open water paddle in higher than 15 mph winds.
- If there is any doubt about proceeding safely, wait a while to see if the conditions improve. Never paddle into questionable conditions simply to stay on schedule.
- Get off the water if you see any lightening.
- Do not paddle in high-powered boat traffic areas.
- Have novice paddlers start by paddling into the wind/current. This way, by the time they are tired, the wind/current will carry them back.
- Plan your trip to include extra time for rest, non-paddling activities, and delays caused by inclement weather.
- Keep things simple.

Chapter 10

Putting It All Together

Flow and the Quality of Life

One of the largest psychological studies ever conducted, concluded that the people who have the most "flow" in their lives are the happiest people on Earth.

A considerable pile of research shows that in the state of "flow" we are more confident, capable and aware and we experience positive transformation, both psychologically and mentally.

Psychologist Mihaly Csikszentmihalyi (who coined the term "flow") says that "flow" is when "every action, movement and thought follows inevitably from the previous one, like playing jazz."

According to the "Flow Genome Project", a trans-disciplinary, international organization, "flow" is technically defined as a peak state of consciousness where we feel our best and we perform our best.

We could keep going on and on about how important "flow" is when it comes to the quality of life.

Flow and Stand Up Paddle Boarding

How is this relevant to stand up paddle boarding?

Science has showed that if some one is taken out of their comfort zone by 4%, they are able to achieve the state of "flow". Yes, 4% is all that it takes. Anything above, may be too much of a challenge and lead to negative results and anything below, may be too little and ineffective.

There are two key points that accompany the concept of the 4% that we need to always keep in mind.

1. It is dependent on and specific to the individual.
2. It can be brought into any activity, whether that is physical, social, mental, psychological, etc.

Looking at stand up paddle boarding we see how easy it is to apply both of these two factors.

For some people the 4% can be simply getting outside, in the heat or the cold and on the water while for others, stand up paddle touring and camping cross country. For some people the 4% can be sitting or kneeling on the board while for others white water stand up paddling.

Either way, it is a fact that the versatility of stand up paddle boarding positively transforms people's lives day in and day out.

On the same note, we have also heard several people say that they tried paddle boarding in the past and did not enjoy it. We believe that this should not be happening and we can only attribute it to poor instruction.

As this activity becomes more and more popular, it is our responsibility as stand up paddle board instructors/guides to bring it in a safe and fun way to as many people as possible.

Code Of Ethics

1. I will always respect the water and the tradition.

2. I will feel responsible and watch out for every life in and on the water:

3. I will always be aware of my surroundings.

4. I will always wear my leash in honor of the fellow paddlers who have died during this sport.

5. I will always commit to the stroke and pull myself towards the blade.

6. If I fall off the board, I will always persevere and get back on the board.

7. I will always look for new places to paddle.

8. I will stand up and paddle every day, even in my mind.

9. I will share my experience and pass on my enthusiasm to non-paddlers.

- *Inspired by surfing legend Shaun Tomson*

Epilogue

A Note from Tim

Water has always been an integral part of my life whether canoeing and skim boarding (at age 7), sea kayaking, white water kayaking, sailing (racing Hobie Cats), scuba diving, stand up paddle boarding, surfing, serving in the Coast Guard (five years) rescue diving and boat operating for law enforcement agencies. It all started growing up on Lake Huron, where I was paddle boarding my first board, a used 7ft 2" Con Butterfly.

Through all my time on or in the water I realized that no matter who you are, water is calling you and sooner or later you are going to answer the call. Stand up paddle boarding is one of the fun and exciting ways to do this!

Happy (Water) Trails To You!

A Note from Vie

I consider myself extremely fortunate to have been born and raised in an environment that values tradition, strength, beauty and the gift of water.

It has been my life-long passion to not only respect and embody these core values but also figure out ways to share them with as many people throughout the world as possible. Stand up paddle boarding is one of the most effective ways I have found that can make this happen.

I welcome you and encourage you to no matter where you are, find a way, to spread the love and change lives, one paddle stroke at a time...

Stay safe!

About the Authors

Vie Binga is a lifestyle entrepreneur, outdoor adventurer and author. She loves to biohack blending science and nature, to enhance physical and mental performance, sharing her findings with others.

She believes that high intention, sincere effort, and intelligent execution will always make an impact in people's lives and the world.

When she is not teaching or writing, she can be found rock climbing, surfing, whitewater kayaking or scuba diving.

Tim Ganley is a lifestyle entrepreneur, outdoor adventurer and author. He loves experimenting with disciplines that lead to physical and mental strength and endurance.

He believes that if people learn about the state of flow and practice building their life around it, the world will be much happier.

When he is not teaching or designing new programs, he can be found white water kayaking, rock climbing, scuba diving, off road biking or surfing.

Valuable Resources

Blog posts: http://AskTimAndVie.com

How-To Videos& Teacher Training Videos:
   YouTube.com/c/AskTimAndVie

We would love to hear from you!

Email: training@asktimandvie.com

Instagram: @ask_tim_and_vie

Periscope: @ask_tim_and_vie

Twitter: @ask_tim_and_vie

Facebook: AskTimAndVie

Website: AskTimAndVie.com

Bibliography

1. http://hawaiihistory.org
2. http://www.surfersjournal.com
3. http://www.surfscience.com
4. http://www.boardlady.com/index.htm
5. http://shauntomson.com/
6. "Tom Blake: The Uncommon Journey of a Pioneer Waterman" – Croul Publications

Made in the USA
San Bernardino, CA
01 December 2016